Floating Across a Life

Personal Poetry and Essays

by

John Burl Artis

featuring

Mycah Leigh Artis

Contents

Chapter One – Words of an Educator

For forty plus years, I have been proud to call myself an educator. Throughout those many years and experiences, emotions and feelings have often been expressed through my poetry.

What follows in Chapter One are the most tantalizing of those poems written over the years, capturing feelings of the moment and those lasting my lifetime.

These poems were often written after a class experience or a year in a leadership experience. The poems range in time from 1968 to 2009.

Enjoy and emote.

Fragile Educator

Today I am aware I may be beyond
where my students can come now.
Who I am isn't even explicable to myself.
I am not an objective teacher.
I teach about life through living it,
not by talking about life.

Education, for me, is subjective and
emotionally oriented.
Seeking the best of myself becomes part of the
act – Teaching by doing and being.
I can see the organic connectedness
between my students and me.
I know for us, knowing the other
will have a profound effect
on my soul.

I see the mystic side of this educator,
but dare I let the mystic out
with soul bared for all to see.
Dare this soul reach out
and see the light of the realistic world?
Is it too fragile,
and my makeup too feeble
to take the attacks of a perverse world?

It's Personal

It almost seemed as if he was reliving an earlier
experience,
touching a familiar cord in his memory.
He glanced around, seeking to focus on the
faces in the audience,
working to clear his mind of a memory of faces
from another time.

Like a warm shaft of sunlight, the memory
insisted on being considered.
It had power independent of his mind.
He asked a question asked by him
a dozen times before.

Turning heads,
contemplating his question,
eyes with varying degrees of aliveness prepared
to respond.
Responses ran the gauntlet from curiosity,
acceptance, dismissal, ridicule, ignoring.
All emotional possibilities staring at him,
eyes turned his way.

Did all of this really make any difference?
What had it mattered that he cared enough to
ask people not to hate?
What difference had his vulnerability made?
What were the changes in society he spoke
about with such passion and enthusiasm?

Who was ever able to live
an inner-directed life? He wondered.
At what juncture did the outside world
insinuate its ugly head into his consciousness?
Had all the exploration of ethics and personal
risk-taking moved people closer together?

The pastor screamed,
"You have not converted a man because you
have silenced him!"
Tis true as both an implicit and explicit message.
To hear the philosophy of another is not to
adapt the philosophy.
Opening the mind of others takes consensual
action, listening and hearing.

Listening and hearing were a first step.
Next was internalizing and acting on the
message,
eliciting a personal lifestyle change.
Such possibility now seemed remote.

Ten long years of questioning, seeking, charting
        the dream.
The dream appeared lost along with his youth.
While the passion of the convictions lived on,
        too many lost battles made the words
        come out empty and hollow by his own
        evaluation.

He thought he could detect a defeated tone.
The fervor of the beliefs still smoldering,
but a new path for their emersion was needed.

For the first time he seriously wondered about
        the need to depart his beloved
        profession.
The thought both depressed and exhilarated
him.

Meandering

Meandering through. Thoughts
reflected backward, forward,
until now merges with then and
the future. Ropes lie along the
pathway for passengers who
need a firm guide – a lamp, an
anchor. Yet, the ropes don't
lead anywhere without passion,
without the sense of purpose
and vision of the dreamer –

Meandering through. The
problems emerge out of the
present, but are filtered
through the prism of the past
solutions, habits, dreams and
frustrations. Thinkers apply
their supplicant powers of
penetration – seeking success
without pain, without
confrontation with the soul

Meandering through. The
dreamer reaches through the
clouds, pushes them aside and
steps off into the thin rarified
air of the uncertain – the
chaotic happening.
The dreamer envisions a newer,
better world, and opens the
door of the vulnerability.

Meandering through. Paths to
be explored – No tabulate
direction identified ahead – but
trusting vision without.

Telling the Future

Transform,
  make anew,
add value,
  seek new knowledge,
    reach the Wisdom of others.

Write
  about what you feel,
what you imagine, and
  let the tale enrich through the telling.

Talk,
  speak words,
add rhymes,
  spread the joy,
    listen to the melody of a child.

Sing,
  about the foils and foibles,
peeks inside, and
  let the notes illuminate through the sound.

Envision,
  picture a preferred future,
stand for a newer world,
  seek the support of others.

Draw,
  provide frameworks
concerning the world anew, and
  invite the light to shine forth through the
living.

On the Wings of Change

Constant: change.
Moments in time,
already a new universe.
Moments lost,
already a fractured Vision.

Constant: hunger.
Food for some,
for others merely starvation.
Affluence guarded,
while others have nothing.

Constant: terror.
Poverty breeds contempt,
contempt encourages aggression.
Protected and gated,
no longer any security.

Constant: difference.
Spread the word,
make a contribution,
add your voice,
take action hallowed,
on the wings of change.

Dreamer

World of make believe,
everyone connecting,
and understanding one another,
without fear.

Touch received as a gesture
of integrity,
ending with its own inertia,
or inviting further explanations of my soul.

Community of learners,
teaching and learning,
sharing openly
Personal Philosophies.

World of make believe,
systems dedicated to an atmosphere
of acceptance.

Lying Here

Lying here, wondering aloud
will the circle open
or
tightly withhold from entrance
those who do not
arrive on this path
with
wealth

Lying here looking out, embracing
a question for answers
beyond the mundane
and
asking for the chance
to lift off the
veil of ignorance

Lying here studying excellence,
asking if excellence
will win out
or again will
powers based
on position and inheritance
stomp out, hold off,
prevent
meritocracy.

Lying here knowing imposters
have but a moment
to protest
before their dream
is snuffed out by the power holders.

Moments

Moments when one looks at one's actions,
asks evaluative questions,
and arrives at some sort of moral position
about meaning and purpose
come rare.
Often, when such moments arrive,
it is because the double life clashes.

A double life is one on the straight and narrow,
meeting the expectations of others,
coupled with one focused on making meaning,
exposing the questions
of hypocrisy and authenticity.
Which life is hypocritical
and which one is authentic
becomes the genesis of the clock.

Actions from either life happens
by happenstance
or by calculated
and knowing choice.
I am alone in the world –
Together with,
and for others.

Moment to Moment

Moment to moment
Those shall,
I will,
They demand,
I do – what?

Demands come forth,
questions arise,
a relative reality emerges,
where they see black,
I see white.

Can I hold fast
to my worldview?
Withstand the pressure
of the profound others,
and act as I wish?

Another System

Another system eagerly received.
Providing structure.
establishing procedures.
which dictate routine,
perpetuating itself
through its own inertia.

A Collection of People

A collection of people
never quite becoming a sharing community,
still feeling like it's more important to
posture and perform than
reach out with love and authenticity.

And the worst part,
they don't even know what they are missing.
They think what they have is all there is,
not knowing life is available in other patterns.
Lust and jealousy still controls them.

They will leave the collective
still hating, taunting, being afraid,
never knowing there is something else,
too frightened to risk
Faith, Hope, or Love.

I grieve for them and fear for me.
While together, we missed so much.
Too bad, we are all less
because of the missed opportunity
Dragged down and crushed
by the lack of a sharing community.

An Obligation

We are what we are willing
   to make ourselves.
Making myself an expert
  means determining how to use the
information.

We are what we are willing
  to do.
Sharing my talents
  becomes an obligation to the whole.

Compromise

Investigation of my soul is my constant
companion.
With my companion I fear whether the word
today is compromise.
Can people really have a life that lets them exist
the
  way they want it to be?
I think so, but I am still unsure.
Do I live this life myself or must I separate
myself
    from the place I love to live a fulfilled life?

Martin Luther King, Jr. said that one can
imprison
  a person's body, but that mind could never
    be imprisoned without the consent of the
mind's owner.
I want to believe that.
However, I wonder what happens when one of
my choices
  runs headlong against what society says I
should do.

Will the pressure from society be too great?
  Will I be able to lead life as I see it?
Is there such a reality as an individual?
How much of what I consider my uniqueness
  is just a conditioned response
    to my environment?

Stamina and Strength

I am considering the meaning of what I do –
What I offer –
What I bring to the table.
I cannot fathom the hatred
that appears to follow what I do.

Nor can I fathom the love
that is generated by what I do.
The excitement of it emerges
from the words I share
is a marvel to behold.

So the emerging question
revolves around my own endurance.
Do I have the stamina and strength
to ward off the hatred
while accepting and nurturing love?

My style and passion
appear to generate
strong emotions.
Can I last?
Can I last?

The Question Before Me

The question before me:
Can I endure?
Ought I acquire?
Would it be a better life?

The question before me:
Change is difficult
and my life is rich
but ought I acquire?

The assumptions of some
speak loudly and sharply.
They say my conduct looks like this,
while I do not recognize the description.

So once again:
Do they speak truth?
or are they reflecting
their own failings?

Can I endure?
Is the vision worth it?
Must I endure
the pain that is inflicted by those who speak?

I ask the question.
Can I be what I am?
Or must I acquire
a false identity?

Close Out the Sound

The sound's screaming in my ear,
the sound of impending disaster.
What brought me here?
What led me to this spot?
Could I have prevented the arrival?

Love or hate,
it has always been this way.
Either warmth and depth
of human emotion,
feeling positive or negative.

With no gray,
its white hot embers,
or the emerald coolness
of the mountain stream
washing over those I touch.

My worldly image
not manageable,
fueled by intensity,
fed by a "can-do" attitude,
unable and unwilling to
wait on those who linger.

Too much the sound again.
I seek peace, solace.
Enough. Too hot.
I cannot go on,
close out the sounds in my ear.

I Am, I Cried

The very essence of what I am has been
challenged.
I now face the ultimate test.
I feel a political struggle brewing.
And I wonder whether my strength of
conviction will be strong enough to do what I
know to be right.
I am, I cried.

We never know when that existential moment,
that moment of choice may be upon us.
We never know when we will have to face
ourselves and say,
Am I real?
Unfortunately, the answer is not always clear.

Such a quest I have.
So much awaits merely my decision.
So much of what I feel
rolls uselessly from my lips only to disappear in
the wind of time,
heard by a few, forgotten by most,
and imprinted on my memory for action – later.

The question I must answer,
the same question every human must
ultimately face:
Will I be true to my soul, or will I
opt out for the good life?
And lose touch with all I really have –
Myself.

I am only certain of one thing now –
I am searching and I will not be deterred
I will at least give myself the chance
to hear my own song, and
to test out the notes to that song of life
tasting my melody.

If doing that means losing the "good life"
so be it.
For as a beautiful book once said,
"What does a man gain if he owns the world,
but loses his own soul?"
I am, I cried.

Introspection

Can I look inside and feel a sense of
accomplishment?
Is my construct a Paradigm of growth or
stagnation?
Have I lost sight of the larger agenda?
Has survival outlived, outfoxed transformation?

When looking sides, the feelings and passion for
a cause are over
       in that box, on the shelf right next to
       risk-taking.
Causes larger than mere economic survival have
been shunted
       aside.

Yet am I not learning? The mind is alive,
Actively seeking new ideas, new dramas, new
paroxysms of
       delight.
Learning is the passion.

So are causes eliminated?
       Left over in that box called youth?
So, can the passion for learning lead to a new
cause?

Chapter Two – Loving

My life is marked by a host of people I have loved and some I continue to love today. The emotional bounty of my love was, for the most part, given freely without the requirement to reciprocate. To love is to live openly through being vulnerable. My loves are represented by such vulnerability and transparency in the poems that follow.

Expectations

Do I really believe my definition of love?
Love as a willingness to give of one's self,
With no need for the love to be returned,
with no expectation that it will be returned.

Faced with those who do not return love,
Do I give as much? Do I offer myself?
Am I open when the openness is not
returned?
Perhaps, I too have expectations for love.

I know it hurts to be rejected
  and I am confused when others do not care.
Is the definition of love in need of revision?
I cannot answer now.

Lonely Will

This is a lonely journey,
  with only the slightest help
from those on the edge,
  unable to view my world.

I can pull them in,
  but cannot burden them with me.

I am the determinant
I am the last line,
I am my world,
I am.

Hard to be me,
but the most exciting thing ever
encountered.

I will,
do all, see all, feel all, touch all.
No limit on my will,
will to be happy! Will to be sad!

Will to know,
  but most important will

Pure and unadulterated
in my command,
fulfilling me, washing over me,
engulfing me
God, are you there?

Human penchant for self knowledge
I see me.
I face my thoughts.
I worship the possibility of touching
  the mystical, the transcendent.

Floating on a high of ecstasy
I experience a moment of connection...
Deep inside I feel the spirit
soaring out, out to the unknown
  and back to grasp me, touch me.

touching the inner most side of my mind,
sliding deeper and deeper
into the murky nature of me.
Why do birds?
What do I seek?

Floating into my dream
touching my moroseness
feeling the melancholy in my soul.
Is there more?
Is this enough?

Love per Chance

The moment she comes near,
the animal hunger emerges,
wanting to touch her,
and be touched by her.

The question also emerges,
would she respond authentically,
would there be any fire,
would her eyes emit boredom.

Whether any warmth emerges
depends on the past,
depends on the present,
depends on human connection.

Enthusiastic response is to me apparent.
Acceptance of the touch,
welcoming lips open to a kiss,
touching eternity.

All this depends on a fragile spark,
a connection of two human beings,
both seeking the appearance of love,
by doing more than pretending.

Can intimacy be nurtured,
from that single moment,
does animal fever turn to romance,
will all attraction die when she speaks?

The moment flames with possibility,
maybe this time there will be more,
maybe this time love has a chance.

Per chance love has a chance,
each one holds onto the hope,
out of this moment comes more,
    even love has a chance.

The Me That Is Me

Hear my plea.
This is all that I ask-
To be understood when I am
understandable,
nurtured where nurturable,
touched when touchable,
and allowed to simply be
wherever I want to be.

Deep in the midst of internal discussion
debating with myself –
wanting to hear my debates as they
intertwine with yours,
unsure of myself,
facing inner turmoil,
needing to feel your love forever
as I enter the me that is me.

The Music

What was said was said no turning back.
Our look is forward, braced only by the music.

The pain is real, words do carry grief,
we are scarred forever,
soothed only by the music.

The world will welcome, one more destruction,
of a family once loving,
embraced only with the music.

The music offers up melancholy,
melodies that touch the soul,
big, bold, brassy sounds, upholding hope –
upholding hope.

Candle of Family Love

How far that little candle throws his beams!
    So shines a good deed in a naughty world.
                    Shakespeare

- The candle of family love –
- coffee and morning in bed,
- acceptance of a brother in our home,
- scratching the ears of a beloved pooch,
- adding a thank you for service received,
- fulfilling a request simply because it's requested,
- fixing a meal as an act of joyful giving,
- light our candle friends to frame conversation.

Greater, Deeper My Love

What beyond myself prepares me
for the journey?
Greater and deeper my love
loving as fully as I can
living as fully as I can
getting outside myself and embracing the
profound.
Greater and deeper my love

My journey beckons me
opening to others
sharing self with others
opening to self – love
changing the way the world is
to a Vision:
I – am – alone – in – the – world –
together with others.

Only Human

He touches me with his poetry.
He touches me with his purity.
He angers me that I am only human.
I can only absorb so much with my limits.
I try to tell him, tell him what I've learned,
 but my words come out cold, twisted,
 somehow missing the meaning.
I tell him I am only human,
only human.

Hallowed Out

Emotionally confused,
faced with perfunctory human contact,
sharing stopped,
friendship and love interrupted.

Essential love for and concern
about people,
trust worthiness reaffirmed,
gift of acceptance.

Challenging intimidation,
coercion and power,
overwhelming emotions-
  unconditional

Old Friend's Lament

Old friends,
you are many and far removed.
I hear your voices when I listen,
I remember your words and your touch.
I appreciate all that you taught me.
I love you now and forever – that's it.

Old friends,
wishing I had the power to reach you,
wishing the misunderstandings
    were cleared away,
wishing your smiles reflected in the glass
    before me,
wishing your full figure filled my arms,
wishing your easy manner filled my day,
wishing you cared enough to call,
wishing you had never left me,
wish you loved me the way I could love you.

Leslie

Listening to one another,
hearing more than was said,
      sometimes saying too much,
backtracking and retreating
from words emerging too soon.

Writing one another,
reading each other's words,
      often sharing a dream,
exposing inner feelings and conflicts,
parts of each person's soul.

Climbing the mountaintop,
plunging to the valley of despair,
      once or twice peeking into the mystical
moving beyond the present reality
which can limit intimacy.

Drawing our bodies together,
curving close to one another,
      capturing the sensation of touch
exchanging energy and the flow
of intimate plateaus.

Grasping the eternal
      holding onto what was given,
      growing because we embrace.
Giving to you the only repayment possible,
my love.

Lenita

Old memories
reawaken after dormancy
remembered with fond anticipation
today will be a day fulfilled
with all the refreshing relish of a walk
back into the past.

Our paths crossed again
mutual learning emerges
insights about what could be
laughter over the simple and complex
walking the challenge together
from the past to the future.

Teresa

So, you don't want me to touch you,
  Okay, so be so –
I never forced the touch,
  Indeed, I always wait until you
      make the first move.

Teresa, I made it clear.
  Touch was my way of relating –
I never required touch,
  nor was I first to touch
      and initiate that first embrace.

Always I ask
  before pulling you into my body space –
  the sanctity of lonely space
Teresa I honor your request, except
  Why couldn't you believe enough in me
      to tell me yourself?

Max

I look inside and see explosive energy
I carefully reach out and caress
the bubble of life force that is there.
I assume there is always more there,
and I am not disappointed.
I ask if I can receive another slice,
and I am abundantly rewarded
with a whole loaf.

Dear friend, you are fast becoming
an anchor for my focal point.
I depend on you and open up
to you, a conscious choice.
I become vulnerable by choice.
I reveal my sustenance by choice.
I gear my soul willingly,
and love the decision I've made.

Even more, I love that my gifts
of myself are received with delicate care.

Don't Run

Don't run!
Face me.
Say to me what you are feeling about me,
about you,
about life or about anything.
I hate mysteries,
and I cannot stand suspense.
If I am a bore, tell me, but for
John's sake,
do not run
and hide,
nor force me
to guess
what
you
are
feeling!

So Far

So far from one another –
Can't quite touch you.
Do you want me?
Feel me?
Reject me?
 or what?

So far apart –
Got to know what's on your mind.
Need a signpost,
a positive marker,
like lovers from the past,
Where are you now when I need you?

Wall

Wall,
created by whom?
Kept in operation
by whom?

Don't know the answer
to either question
I know I tried my best,
not good enough.

Wall still there,
staring at me,
daring me to butt
my head.

"No touch."
"Why?"
"Because I'm afraid."
"Of what?"

Wall again!
Fear rises up,
blocks the touch,
keeps me from reaching you.

Separation

What happened?
How did it come to this?
Could the pain be real?
How could she say goodbye?

Mind racing over the rivers
of the past,
searching for clues about
what happened and why?
Hard to acknowledge the end.

Wondering about the slips,
little slips of the tongue,
spoken innocently, but
with meaning far beyond
the tiny words.

Remembering what it was like
in the beginning,
but knowing those times no longer live,
buried in memory forever.

What happened? Life.
How did it come to this? Neglect.
Could the pain be real? Most definitely.
How could she say goodbye? By imitating me.

<u>Trust</u>

An elusive concept,
born of faith in the goodness
of others.
Often naïve at the onset,
while easily destroyed.

A painful journey,
through human nature
or is it nurture?
How can one trust
if human nature is
untrustworthy?

Marred by the work of the cynics,
those who trust
often threaten the worldview
of those who would see
greed behind every action.

Trust, conceptually dangerous,
yet without
there can be no love
no human progress,
no unity,
no growth.

In the Moment

In the moment,
I have lived, loathed, loved.
In the moment,
I have thought of death
In this moment,
life won out.

So now I face self examinations
Can I find the path
away from self loathing?
Can the devils that rule my thought
be cauterized and rubbed out?
Can I recognize that sense of life?

This I know,
the only answer to my loathing
is love.
Self love,
  love of others
    but most importantly, love.

Love doesn't just appear,
love must be earned.
Earned by self acceptance –
I am what I am
warts and all
so I am I cried.

I am a part of the human universe
so nothing human is foreign,
including what I do.

Thus my actions are what they are –
 Human actions
  by a human being
      living

Chapter Three – Essays in the Key of Life

There are expressions that demand a full linguistic approach.   The following essays, written again over a broad span of time, mark a different way of looking at my life.

Essay One, "Adult Language", indirectly about my mother, and perhaps all mothers.

Essay Two, "Ned-An Uncommonly Free Man," about a man from my childhood who influenced me more than he will ever know.

Essay Three, "A Life Changing Experience: How a "Heart Incident Alters a Man's Life View," written fourteen years ago, describes in detail a 'Heart Incident' and its aftermath.

Essay Four, "Save the Life of My – Me!", a series of thoughts about love and loving written over thirty years ago.

Essay Five, "Latitudes and Attitudes," a highly personal free form exploration to per chance inspire and intrigue.

Adult Language

We stood by the place where she once stood.
The place was surrounded by a grove of hickory,
birch, and maple trees. It was half way up a
hilly area of the farm. From the site we looked
on a ravine cut into two banks with thick woods
by a small creek of rushing, frigid water. The
water was clear with a rocky bottom open to
view and trout swimming in the midst of the
water.

We touched our hands together at the sight of
this place and slowly began to weep. Our tears
were not merely shed in pain and remorse. We
also wept for the lost thoughts she had held so
strongly as she gazed down this same ravine,
touching and drinking the frigid water of the
creek.

When we were children, Momma would go to
this place often. Upon her frequent returns
from this spot, we would see that far away look
in her eyes. Then we would know she was
somewhere else, somewhere we could not go
with her. That far away look could last for
hours.

"Momma, where do you go when you return
from up there?" we would ask. "Oh, to a place
so far away and yet so near too," she would say.
"Don't you know Mommas have special places
where they can go to escape the harsh voices of

the day and the hard times we are suffering through?"

And then, she would stop talking and look toward us with tears in her eyes. She would then say, "Momma loves you more than life itself. You know that don't you?"

We would nod our heads and run toward the door, not at all certain what she meant. We were pretty certain she was speaking adult language. We didn't know that language.

We knew we were poor. We knew sometimes we were hungry. But we also knew Momma was there for us, right by our side ready to steady us if we started to fall. *We* knew all that, but adult language about love forever, no, we didn't know about that yet.

Looking back after running out the old ratty door of the house, we would often see her reach out her hand and softly weep as she watched us. Her hair hung loosely down in its jet black splendor and her soft bosom heaved with tears. She moved her hand as if to catch us before we fell. She was so beautiful.

Today, we laid her to rest. With her ashes, we honored her last wish to float in the air forever, fling free down that ravine and on into the creek. Ashes to ashes, she was now free to float softly toward all those places she used to travel to in her mind when she started down the ravine – places she never saw in person but always imagined.

Good-bye dear Momma. Wish we could have known all of those adult thoughts you had up here in this special place. Wish we could have known that man who left you and us behind when we were little children. Wish you would not have been so lonely all those years. Wish we could talk with you, Momma, one more time using adult language. We understand such knowledge now. Farewell Mamma.

Ned – An Uncommonly Free Man

Teachers, parents, and administrators often hear a cry in the spring of the year from seniors, "I can't wait to graduate!" or "I get out of this prison on June 9th!" or, "Free at Last. No more listening to the rules or having to answer to mom. No one will tell me what to do now."

Recently, I experienced this lament firsthand when my daughter graduated from high school. As I watched her go through the experiences of graduation and test her theories of freedom, I wondered just how clear her and her peers' understanding of the nature of freedom and independence truly was.

As I pondered the core of freedom, I thought about how independence and absolute responsibility for one's self is not an easy journey. Freedom and independence of self takes a keen awareness of who you are and explicit acknowledgement of your capabilities and limitations. The essence of freedom involves an understanding of personal needs, and an understanding of what constitutes luxuries of want, not need.

Being independent, free, and responsible, therefore, means articulating and fulfilling one's needs. It means not being trapped into a mad scramble towards the acquisition of luxuries – luxuries which create conformity, not freedom.

Understanding the difference between needs and wants, and fulfilling those needs while controlling the wants, is the key to managing life.

The above words are abstractions or ideas, and do not take on real meaning until a real person is experienced and described for consideration. I discovered just such a person when I returned to my childhood home a few years ago. There, I discovered Ned, a man I had known as a child. Through three days of observations of Ned, I discovered what kinds of choices this man made and continues to make to live a life of freedom based on independence and personal responsibility. Let me tell you the story of those three days.

Ned is a rather comical looking little man. In keeping with the custom of the men of this area of Central Wisconsin, Ned wears his trousers very low on his hips. While observing him walk, sit, squat, or even crawl under a vehicle, I became aware of the real possibility he might lose those trousers at any second. Additionally, the trousers are always covered with grease and other accumulated dirt from the farm or his shop. His shirt is generally faded blue or worker green with a string attached to his tobacco sac hanging out of one shirt pocket.

Ned can be found normally working on about a four-day beard, thus giving his face a permanent scraggily look. He only has one eye (He lost the other eye in a machine shop accident), and that one eye has a dark brown center with a clear white outer rim, opening very wide when he looks at another person or while he is talking. There is a curious, intriguing mixture of pain and merry twinkle mirrored in that face and one good eye.

Topping off Ned's appearance is an old floppy hat, coated with grease and dirt, long since having lost any elasticity it ever had. The hat sits on the side of Ned's head and is always in danger of falling off. The hat is worn everywhere Ned goes. Even in the house, the hat can be found plopped atop Ned's head as he eats a sandwich or watches a little television.

The final descriptive touch for gaining the full physical measure of this man is the way he looks when he speaks. Ned is a smoker, and all of his life, he has rolled his own cigarettes. At any given time, Ned generally has a cigarette dangling out of the corner of his mouth. Consequently, when he speaks, the words flow out of the other corner of his mouth, raised open for the occasion.

Ned lives on a farm approximately five miles from Wonewoc, Wisconsin. However, by no stretch of the imagination can he be called farmer. Despite raising a large garden, caring for four or five head of cattle for milk and meat for the family, and planting a portion of the 80-acre farm with crops, he does not describe himself, nor does anyone who knows him, describe him as a farmer.

In fact, Ned does lots of different types of work, but none of the work captures who he is as a person. Ned built a house on the land where he lives, but he is not a carpenter. The house, Ned will tell you, is for Dorothy, his wife, and it took almost seven years to finish. On the farm, Ned created a lake and stocked it with fish he and his children caught. Yet Ned could not be called an environmentalist or biologist. The lake is beautiful, but creating and caring for the lake is just a hobby for Ned. Ned builds tractors and tractor motors, boats and boat motors, wagons and wagon accessories, and fish smokers. Yet, in each case, he applies his creative genius to the work as a hobby, not a profession.

Ned is an uncommonly gifted man with an insatiable curiosity that leads him to try many tasks and accept many challenging situations. Throughout his life and his acceptance of the many challenges, his central goal is to provide the opportunity for him and his family to live their lives beholden to no one and in splendid isolation from society's demands, in comfort, and with their needs met. While accomplishing this goal, Ned depends on his family, but no one else. He is a 'Renaissance Man' with interests and skills relating to many trades or professions and a master of his own fate. Life, with all its surprises and frailties, is met on his terms, and Ned accommodates himself to those terms to ensure his independence from the opinions of other men. He is one of the freest men I have ever met.

The last time I visited Ned at his farm home, it was well over twenty-five years since he last saw me.   When I left Wisconsin, I was barely in my teenage years. My personal memories flooded my mind prior to the visit, and I remembered this funny-looking little man always plodding around working on a new invention in his machine shop. As I approached the farm, I wondered to myself how everything would look now. Would Ned still be the same little man trying a new hobby or looking to invent a new tractor? Would he have given in to the pressures of the world and now be working at a steady job for the income?

I eased the car down the tiny gravel road that led up to Ned's house. Flashbacks of my father, now dead, and Ned's description of my father flooded my consciousness in the few moments it took me to maneuver down the driveway. My father was always driven at what he did. He worked hard all of his life. When he was living on the farm nearby to Ned's he was always up by 4:30am, finished milking his 30-40 herd of cows by 6:00am, returned to the house and finished breakfast by 6:30am, and by 6:45am, he would be back in the barn and farmyard finishing the daily chores related to running a dairy farm. In the spring, summer, or fall, my father would often work well into twilight, getting crops planted, gathering crops, putting up hay for the winter, or managing the fields for the next year to come.

Ned, of course, never took farming that seriously. He certainly had no intentions, even as a young man, of ever getting up at 4:30am in the morning to do something he didn't even enjoy. For Ned, milking was finished when it was finished, not on a time schedule. He once described my dad as someone with a terrible sickness called "Get-up-itis," and he intended to stay away from my father until it was determined if the disease was catching.

There was another memory too that quickly flooded my mind. This second memory was of a cold, snowy winter's night when we got a desperate telephone call from Dorothy, Ned's wife. She said Ned was hurt bad down in his machine shop and would we come quick. The snow was nearly two feet deep from the long evening snowfall, and the roads were filled too high with snow for a trip to Ned's in a car. So my father and older brother bundled up, took along shovels, and started off on the tractor to make the cold midnight run over to Ned's farm – a trek of approximately four miles by road.

When they arrived, they found Ned holding his severed eye in his hand with blood oozing out all around the eye. Ned had been welding for one of his inventions when a piece of metal, white-hot, flew up and into his eye. When Dad arrived, he found Ned weak and in need of emergency care.

Dorothy had already called the local doctor only to find he was out of town. Quickly, Dad called our house and instructed my older brother to drive the car down to the end of the main road and wait for them. Dad and my brother brought Ned out to the main road on the tractor and then got him into the car. In the wee hours of the night, Dad and one of my brothers sped off to Madison, Wisconsin (nearly 70 miles away) and emergency care for Ned.

Ned lost his eye that night long ago. Now, as I rolled close to him, I saw this little man with the floppy hat squint with his good eye to see who was in the car. I stopped the car, opened the door, and crawled out of the driver's seat and said, "Hello Ned, do you know who I am?"

He squinted carefully, and after a moment's hesitation, a smile crossed his face, the cigarette moved to the corner of his mouth, and he said, "Why of course I know who you are. You are Ralph and Kittie's boy, You are John." Just that quickly, we were friends again.

As the day progressed, Ned and I reminisced about those twenty-five years since I last saw him. So much had changed in my life, but his seemed still focused on the simplicity of fulfilling his needs and pursuing his ideas and hobbies. I asked him about his little lake and how it came in to being. He told me he simply dammed up his spring and let the underground flow emerge to form his lake. This spring was four miles away from the hole that was now the lake, yet simple attention to a little mathematics and some engineering skills led to the creation of Ned's lake.

To stock the lake, Ned didn't depend on outside resources. Instead, each time Ned went fishing, which was quite often, he simply caught, transported, and released whatever fish were caught into his new lake. He told me his lake now had crappies, blue gill, a few walleye, one or two northern pike, and several very large brown trout.

I asked Ned if I could go fishing in his lake. He said yes and told me he would get out his motor, and I could take out the boat. I followed Ned down to the lakeshore to what I assumed was a dock. He opened a little building and took out a tiny motor. I looked around and asked about the boat, but Ned just smiled, walked to the end of the dock and attached the motor to the dock. Then he pulled out two electric cords, attached them to the motor and to a battery and said, "Okay, she's ready to sail."

Amazed, I stepped upon the dock and found it was a floating platform laced tightly to empty barrels. There was railing all the way around with a gate at each end so one could fish off the end. Smiling broadly, Ned shoved me off from the shore and said, "Now that motor isn't fast, but she is steady. Be careful out there with the weeds underwater. If you get caught up in the weeds, well, you will just have to get out."

As I watched Ned walk back up toward the house, I kept thinking about his statement – "If you get caught in the weeds, you'll just have to get out." What a profound description of life itself. Life is met most successfully when each event and personal situation is met with a steady pace focused on "getting out" of the difficult. Events, problems, and periods of depression have a way of working out for those who meet each such occurrence with patience, understanding of what their limits are and what they can do, and with an ultimate acceptance of personal responsibility for each choice and action.

When we tangle our lives in the weeds, there really is no one to get us out. Our lives are solitary moments filled with challenges and predicaments and the only person who can get us "out" or "through" the challenges is ourselves. Whatever we start carries with it the potential for entanglements, and whether we work through those entanglements or abort the effort is ultimately our decision. Others cannot and ought not make those decisions for us.

Life is ours to live. We can choose to exist, to soar, or to abort our personal dreams. We can allow another to decide for us how we will live, but responsibility for doing so still lies with each one of us. The choice determines whether we are free and responsible or we are dependent and irresponsible. For Ned, the choices he made all of his life made it possible for him to be an uncommonly free man.

A Life Changing Experience: How a "Heart Incident" Alters a Man's Life View

The bright August sunlight poured through the windows of the van as my wife maneuvered down the road toward Interlochen, Michigan. My youngest daughter dazed fitfully in the middle seat of the van. She is not a good traveler, and the tape my wife and I were listening to in the tape deck certainly did not excite her.

I leaned back in my seat and listened to the tape with one ear while also wondering how I got to this spot in my life. The tape, you see, was about how to enhance my healthy food intake by ingesting algae pills. Algae pills! My God, how did I get to this spot?

This saga began on July 20, 1996. That morning I awoke early and got up to quickly run to the bank prior to shopping with my family. I had just returned from a whirlwind ten-day tour of such Midwest hotspots as Chicago, Burlington, Iowa, Sullivan, Illinois, Detroit, Cincinnati, back to Chicago, and back to Detroit. I was a little tired that morning, but also very pleased to be home.

The trip to the bank was a bit of an adventure. When I arrived, there was the normal long line of cars with occupants waiting to deposit their hard-earned money. There were the usual two tellers handling the line. As I sat in my car, I lit a cigarette – something I rarely do at home. The first drag of the cigarette led to an immediate reaction from my body. My heart rate sped up very fast. Puzzled, I threw the cigarette out the window and worked hard to relax.

Finally I finished my banking business and headed home. My heart rate settled down after a good ten minutes of fluttering. I was still feeling strange as I drove home to pick up the family.

After arriving home, I picked up the rest of the family for our trip. My wife and I have three children – two daughters of our own and a "daughter-niece" we took custody of five years ago. We headed to complete several errands including a stop at Lou's pet store, the shopping mall for new shoes, and several other brief sojourns to various suburban stores.

Throughout the two-hour trip, I felt a strange nervous fluttering in my heart. Periodically, my heart rate would speed up for two- or three-minute intervals. I was feeling kind of nauseous, somewhere between wanting to vomit and needing a glass of water. I finally told my wife I needed to go back to the car and wait for her and the children to finish their shopping.

As I headed toward the car, my youngest daughter said she wanted to go with me. She was eight years old at the time and very concerned about health issues. Due to commentary by her big sister, she had recently learned that I smoke occasionally, and she wanted to talk to me about this new discovery. As we walked toward the car, she talked to me about the terrible health evils of smoking and urged me to stop this habit – even occasionally.

We arrived at the van. I opened the door and Mycah (youngest) and I took seats in the van. As we sat waiting, the fluttering feelings began to return. My heart was racing and slowing down, racing and slowing down. Finally, I told Mycah she better go get her mom and sister because Daddy wasn't feeling well.

Just as my daughter got out of the car to go find her mother and sister, they appeared. Now I had a dilemma. I didn't want to tell my wife everything that was happening to me. I thought if I could just get home and rest a little while, I would be okay. So, rather than tell her everything, I told my wife I had a bad case of indigestion and really needed to rest. I asked if we could skip lunch for now and go home.

The late July afternoon dragged on into the three o'clock hour. After returning from the shopping mall and resting for about an hour, I asked if anyone wanted to go with me to have a late lunch. My two daughters immediately said yes. My wife decided to beg off and go for a walk instead.

At approximately four o'clock, my two children and I finished our late lunch at one of our favorite Greek restaurants. The restaurant is in a small shopping mall attached to St. John's Hospital on the corner of Mack and Seven Mile in Detroit. The two girls asked if they could go to a nearby specialty store. I told them to go ahead, I was going to pay the bill and then join them.

I finished paying the bill and started to walk the short distance to the food store. Suddenly, my heart did a kind of flutter as if it had literally turned over in my body. The pace of the heart rate was extremely fast, and I began to fell a kind of fullness across my chest like a liquid had been poured into the chest cavity. I stopped walking and leaned against a wall hoping to force calmness through my body.

After several moments passed, things began to settle down. I knew I needed some medical attention, but my plan was to get the girls, walk back to the van, return home, and then talk with Julie, my wife, to determine our next steps. I decided to walk in to the food store and find the girls.

When I arrived at the food store, my two daughters were just coming out of the entrance. At that moment, my heart took off. I could feel my heart racing at breakneck speed. I was extremely dizzy and started to lose my ability to focus my vision. I stopped my two daughters and told them I needed to sit down in one of the chairs outside the store. I sat down and while struggling to control my bodily feelings, I let the girls know I was not feeling well.

After a few minutes, I attempted to stand up thinking I needed to get home and get to a doctor. I took three or four steps and knew I wasn't going to make it home. Turning to my daughters, I said "Sloane and Mycah, Daddy needs help. You will have to get someone to help me."

My daughters were 12 and 8. Their reaction to my request for help was nothing short of amazing. They quickly ran back into the store and informed the person at the counter to call 911. With that accomplished, they came back outside the store. I pulled some change out of my pocked and sent my older daughter to a telephone to call my wife and tell her to get a ride to the mall to pick up the girls and our van. My youngest daughter stayed with me and held my hand while I attempted to calm down.

When Sloane returned from calling her mom, I told both girls to get a security guard. My thoughts were if I had to leave before my wife arrived, I wanted someone official to be with the girls while they waited for my wife. Instead, they found a nurse who was on her lunch break and brought her to me.

I was admitted to St. John's Hospital Emergency Room at approximately 5:30 pm on July 20th. For the next three hours, the medical personnel fought to lower my heart rate. Periodically, my heart jumped to 180 beats a minute. During one such episode, I asked if I was having a heart attack. The answer was "No, but if we don't get this heart rate under control, you will have one."

At 8:45 pm, I was admitted. This was on a Saturday. Late evening, a doctor appeared to discuss what they thought was going on with me and what the next steps would be. I was told I did not have a heart attack. My condition was described as an arrhythmic heart. I needed to have an angiogram to determine whether there might be a blockage in my heart or some other damage. I would meet the doctor who would perform the "Invasive Procedure" on Sunday morning.

On Tuesday morning, July 23rd, Dr. Robert Cleary performed my angiogram. Early that morning, the nurses prepared me for the event. Lots of body hair was shaved from strategic places, followed by several shots of various medications fed to me intravenously to relax me for the upcoming procedure. At 9:45 am, I was wheeled into a room filled with various sundry machines of modern medicine and no heat! The table I was moved onto was as ice cold.

The procedure began with Dr. Cleary telling me what would happen. He said I might feel a slight sting when they cut into the vein and I might feel the warmth of the dye that would be sent through my heart during the initial angiogram. Even though I was medicated, I was still feeling a great deal of anxiety at this moment. I remembered an earlier telephone call from my older brother who told me how very uncomfortable he had been when they shot the dye into him. I tensed up thinking this was going to be a very painful experience.

As my tension built, I opened my eyes to see Dr. Cleary standing beside of me asking me if I wanted to know the results. I had felt nothing! Yet he was finished with the angiogram and ready to share the results. He said to me, "You have some blockage in one of the minor arteries that feeds the heart, but we can fix it. The question is what do you want?"

I asked, "What happens if you don't fix it?"

His answer was, "You probably will have a heart attack."
I said, "Fix it."

He said, "Okay."

Unbeknown to me, he left the room at this time to talk to my wife. Unlike me, she of course had dozens of questions including how they would fix my heart, what were my chances afterward, and what exactly could I expect as a result of the procedure. During the course of the conversation, the doctor informed Julie there was a 5-12% chance they could cause a heart attack with the procedure (angioplasty) itself. She asked him if I knew that.

He answered, "I am not sure he does know."
She said, "Go back in there and tell him."

Well, Dr. Cleary did tell me. He said, "I need you to be aware that there is a 5-12% chance we could cause a heart attack with this procedure. Do you still want to do it?

I looked at him and said, "You said if I don't do the procedure, I will probably have a heart attack, right? He nodded. I said, "Well, then do it."

As it turned out, my "Invasive Procedure" was not so simple. First, after performing the angioplasty, the physicians discovered my arteries would not remain open. Therefore, they had to place a stent implant in my heart. Second, when I returned to my room, I went into severe pain. I was rushed back into the operating room and a second catheterization was performed. After a very prolonged and delicate procedure, Dr. Cleary found several tiny blood vessels with blockage and performed the angioplasty procedure on them.

Late that evening, I found myself lying in the hospital bed wondering what was next. I could not move and had sandbags laying over the area where the doctors had cut into my groin. I experienced a life-changing event. Yet at that moment, what I did not know was whether I would emerge from this hospital bed at all, and if I did, would I be better off or worse than when I was admitted.

Eighteen hours after the procedure, my nurse came into my room and indicated I could get out of bed. She carefully supported me as I eased up and swung my legs over the edge of the bed. As I did so, the bandage in my groin area turned bright red. I had broken loose and was bleeding. The nurse stepped to the door and yelled, "I need help now!"

She quickly returned to me and ripped off the bandage. She grabbed the blood vessel above the incision point and clamped it shut with her hands. By this time, other hospital personnel had arrived to help. They worked together to stop my bleeding, return me to my bed, re-bandage the groin area, and return the sand bags.

To talk about fear at this point is an understatement. In less than 24 hours, I had experienced the angiogram, two angioplasties, a stent, and now my own blood pumping out of my body. While I trusted the medical care I was receiving, I no longer trusted my own body. I was in true panic. Would I live became a very serious question.

I did live. I left the hospital and began my rehabilitation process. The August car trip in question was my first venture away from our house and marked the beginning of a saga that has continued since then, with many ups and downs and lots to learn and unlearn in my life. What I have discovered about myself and my world since going through the above experience is phenomenal. Truly, I am a different person since those hot days in late July and that first car trip in August.

Let me describe the difference with a list. As a result of those ten months of my life:

- I lost 38 pounds.
- My diet included everything on the infamous food pyramid every day including 12-14 carbohydrate servings a day;
- I stopped smoking;
- I exercised 35-40 minutes at a health club six days a week;

- I read nutrition labels as I shop for food;
- I took four medications a day;
- I worked every day to learn how to relax, control my stress, and get my needed rest;
- I severely reduced my work schedule, cutting back from 65-70 hours a week to approximately 50 hours a week; and
- Every day, I sought that spiritual side of life in an attempt to add to my own wholeness.

Heart disease is no joking matter. For people like me, it is the number one health risk we face. I found out I was a prime candidate at age 50. I am male. At the time of my incident, I smoked, worked far too many hours, and ate far too many restaurant meals. Additionally, my father, mother, and brother, along with several aunts and uncles all died of heart attacks. I also did not exercise regularly before the incident in July.

Today, I believe in a brighter future. My body is in better shape now than in July 1996. I still struggle with lots of feelings, and I still must keep working on centering my thoughts to keep calm. But, I am making progress! And every time I get discouraged, I remember four things that helped me during my ten-month rehabilitation.

First, I think of my wife. She too had a heart incident on July 20, 1996. Her world became very different as a result of my incident. She didn't physically have a heart incident, but she felt everything that happened to me, experienced every pain, and was faced with every decision. I don't want her to ever have to experience any more pain on my account.

Second, I thought of my children. As I said earlier, I have three daughters who were 16, 12 and 8 at the time. I was very interested in seeing them through college and to a point where they would be well-established in their lives. They knew their daddy had a health problem, but they also know I was seriously working toward good health. I like that they know this.

Third, I remembered a remark my brother-in-law said to me in the hospital. When he came to visit me prior to the angiogram, he read me the riot act. In no uncertain terms, he told me, I had to change my life because I owed it to my family and myself. He said I had to exercise and had to quit smoking. Then, with tears in his eyes, he leaned down, kissed me, and said, "I love you brother."

Finally, whenever I get discouraged, I remember a story a nurse told me when I was leaving the hospital. She told me of a woman who had been admitted twenty-five times for various heart procedures. I asked her why, and she answered, "Because she refused to take responsibility for getting better."

I took that responsibility. It was not easy, but the alternative was worse. I remembered what W.C. Fields had placed on his tombstone…"Frankly, I'd rather be in Philadelphia." In my case, frankly, I wanted to be with Julie, and my three lovely daughters, Ried, Sloane and Mycah. To all of them I say, "Thank you for being there, and I am still working hard to be there with you."

Save the Life of My --- Me!

When I listen to that old song from Simon and Garfunkel days, I hear them plead "Save the life of my child cried the desperate mother." Listening and reflecting, I come to realize I am the "child." I am every child whose mother looked out onto the world and cried for help to raise that child, seek meaning for that child, and most of all, protect that child so he can grow to be loved and a lover.

Truly, I am coming to accept that part of my story more and more. With my mother's blessed love, my life was saved in order to give love. My journey through this life is marked by love and loving experiences. Welcome to all who wish to share in those loving experiences.

Come along on the journey as a fellow lover. Come and join me in that search for loving experiences. To you who wish to join in the journey, I say welcome aboard sister, brother, fellow seeker, lover.

I love. I do not choose other roles, for you see, to do so would be to destroy the best in me – my gentleness. I want you to come along for the journey, but I will not force you. I love you. It's that simple because I learned to love by loving myself. And then, I can let my love engulf you too!

Dear old friends. You are many and far removed. I hear your voices when I listen to the love notes inside. I remember your words and your gentle touch. I appreciate all each one of you taught me. I love you now and forever and that's it.

Wishing I had the power to reach you.
Wishing the "misunderstandings"
    were cleared away
Wishing your smile reflected in my glasses
Wishing the fullness of your life
    filled my arms.
Wishing your easy manner filled my time.
Wishing you cared enough to call.
Wishing you had never left me.
Wishing you loved me the way I loved you.

The soul of the iceberg is emerging. I am pushing inside and I know the beginning stops are the easy ones. Peeking into a life and taking the time to experience the depths is an experience in intensity. I am going to need help, and I don't mind telling you dear friends, I need you.

I cannot compete with you, nor do I want to be your teacher, for I have not enough knowledge or wisdom. I will not rule over you for I demand my own freedom of will and only through granting you the same can I be granted such freedom.

Therefore, I am left with only one choice for our journey together – to be your lover, to be connected, to care as one. Can you dig it? Can you let me in? Will you be able to cope? Do you too recognize the multiplicity of love? Do you understand that my loving you only ensures I will be even more capable of loving others, and my love of those others will make your gifts even more unique to me by comparison?

Latitudes and Attitudes

The mind is an amazing instrument. The whole world is contained in my mind. Others exist, but only to the extent that I choose to let them come into my consciousness. I am the world. I control what I think, what I consider truth, what I decide is right or wrong, or what I will do with the days of my life.

Of course the larger society can enter into and influence my world. Society can attempt to force onto me a whole new idea of what reality is. Even so, I can decide to reject that idea and perhaps accept being called an eccentric. I could resist the world's view and become a hermit or I could do my own thing and ignore the dictates of society.

Whatever choice I make, I must accept the responsibility for what my life will be like. Illnesses and natural calamities can alter my decisions, but even so, my decisions are mine to make. I truly am the world. I accept the responsibility of my world with awe, fear, foreboding, anticipation, excitement, and genuine humility.

I am unique. I have characteristics that take me to territory never experienced by anyone else in quite the same way before. I am capable of thinking and contemplating the deeper valleys of my soul.

The meanings of existence are within me. They exist and develop and grow even more concrete and visible because those meanings are challenged by me, by others of significance, by readings, by experiences, by touch, and by the heartaches of the world. Existence – the identification of purpose for the whole of the world. All of that has and is developing inside of me and it simply bursts forth in great gobs, looking for a spot to land.

From out of one – one – that is all there is – I am totality of all that ever was or will be. If I don't learn from that totality, it is forgotten.

And of course, there are millions of "I's" making up the entire world. They each choose what the world will be and what it is. These millions can choose to connect or to separate. No matter whatever they choose, their will will be done.

Charlie Rich wails away, Country Charlie, you got some real heavy down-home sounds that stir the country boy residing in the sophisticated city dweller. All the education in the world can never wipe away the far away joy of a little boy running after a collie dog. The collie dog was running fast to round up the cows to return them to the barn in the late afternoon.

The little boy yells down from on top of the hill they called Old Smokey, "Hey Dad, we found Blackie. She is back here in the bushes. Come on Shep, get that old cow out of there. The little boy yelled again, "Bang, bang, you're dead." The greatest gunfighter in the world just rid the world of the awful William Blackie, the cow. How proud everyone was.

"What's that? Oh yeah, I'm coming Dad. Come on Blackie." Dad, did you hear me? Tears flow – I love you Dad. Dear old man, you would be proud. I'm doing okay Dad. I am making a difference in this world. Dad, your fierce dream to see your son educated and changing the world would be fulfilled.

I like me and who I have become right now. I approve of my actions, and you dear Dad would approve too. Thank you for loving me so much!
                          . . .
"Truth, in my belief, is something which occurs when actions take place: not when phrases are contrived," said Jonathon Kozol. Dare to live the truth. Put your convictions to the test. Put your convictions to the test. Reach out and become a part of the ever flowing river of truth deducing love. If you believe something to be true, put it to the test by acting on that belief immediately and consistently.

...

"A young man is going to have to die in certain ways in order to become the kind of man he needs to be," says Paulo Fraire. Choices are on the line. To make the choices, I must let a little bit of me die. Choices.

Nothing is real, including the awful pain of little children starving all around, including the bullets fired by those children of the poor at one another (I make two hundred times more than my father made in his best year); including the rats that attack the little baby (we kill snakes off); including the multitrillion dollar defense budget for last year (guns don't kill, people do); including the sale of many billions worth of weapons (at General Electric, progress is our most important product); nothing is real! Come out and aide me. Give me strength to resist the crimes of a materialistic apathy. Thoughts to live by...

...

"You and I are different. You ask why, get an answer, and ask why again. Me, on the other hand, I just ask why. That's enough."

God, am I so different? Is what I ask of people so unusual? I see the world and its pain, and I ask people to go beyond the obvious, to search their own soul, to see that all people bleed the same, to risk a touch, to express real concern for those who lose in this world, to be willing to

83

commit to a cause – an ideal, to be fully human.
I cannot believe that others cannot feel what I
feel, understand what I understand, want to
change what I want to, or love as I love.

...

Life is personal. Life and pain is personal.
Bullets are personal. A closed fist is personal.
Words tossed around intending to hurt others
are personal. Spitting on another is personal.
Stealing is personal. Learning to hate is
personal.

Learning about myself is personal. Loving
myself and loving others is personal.
Demonstrating courage and standing for a
principle is personal. Being personal is what life
is all about. I am personal because I am alive as
fully as I can possibly be. I am personal.

...

Old friend, I say to myself, you talk of the need
for simplicity and spiritual reconnecting with
the earth itself. We shared our guests and then
moved to new territory exploring messages
regarding research and mystical action.

The discussion pushed boundaries regarding
feelings about the abstracting process of
research. They, the researchers, must kill the
humanity of their topic in order to be able to

work their own peculiar specialization. They must be "neutral" and "logical" when the situation under investigation cries out for emotion. They must objectify while children continue to starve. They must be an "apolitical" while the world burns around them. They must divorce ethics from research and thus divorce their own humanity from their actions.

Thus it is. In order to function, the researchers, the scientists, kill off the poetry of life for the sake of the experiments on rats.

Old friend, whatever you choose, I support your actions, if those actions please you. Soar and live to the hilt. Enjoy the mysticism of life itself. If per chance that leads you toward research, well then so be it. You I will always love, but I don't have to love your actions, nor do you mine. We understand that too, I think. Keep reaching.

...

Family musings... It was Christmas Eve after lunch. Mother and I went out in the country near Arthur, Illinois, to a country store run by the Amish. While there, I bought a wide brimmed Amish dress hat. It was coal black and an absolute gas!

While on this little adventure I found out from Mother than my great grandfather was not only a prisoner if Andersonville Prison during the Civil War, but that the family has a record of his imprisonment preserved for years. Mother and the family members had gotten a copy of those records for me.

Latitudes and attitudes keep me awake at night. Musings tie me together into a whole, giving me a chance to make sense of it all.

Chapter Four – The Dream Lives On

Poetry became a way of expression for me when a boy. Poetry is still the way I get out repressed or creative whispers in my soul.

My daughter, Mycah, follows this same pathway. Her talent as a writer of poetry and creative non-fiction, an actress, a singer, a director, producer, and quick witted commentator about all that surrounds her emerges as a major life force.

The following poems and creative non-fiction essay written by Mycah Leigh Artis feature wit, descriptive power, and enormous emotion. As you read, Dear Reader, count on seeing much more from this talented lady in the near future.

Burst Bounty

My heart is not American.
Never will it be seduced by Uncle Sam's beard.
Nor does it swell upon hearing
ballads boasting of the land of the free
from sea to shining sea.

My nose is also not American.
It does not relish the smell of perfectly sculpted
meat patties grilling on the 4th of July
   and on that note,
my eyes are not impressed with the firework
displays either.

The touch of an American flag to my fingertips
does not send a prickle, or shiver,
   or tingle down my arm,
unaffected is my skin by the fabric's symbolism.

My appendix, however, is American,
shamelessly excessive like Uncle Sam and
   his yearly parades.
I mean, do human beings really need a second
stomach?

The Couple

I always walk with my father
as my mother tears ahead,
thighs swishing together on high,
fueled by her almost annoyance
at her perpetually lonely walk.
We stroll together at his slow, yet deliberate pace,
commenting occasionally on my mother's behavior,
swapping complaints laden with identical sarcasm.
We watch as she propositions my sister,
trying to find a pace ally as I am to my father,
pretending to be unruffled by my alleged snub.
She shoots me heavy glances,
attempting to entice me away
like a spurned woman showcasing her lack of loss.
But I always walk with my father,
parallel in pace,
because like him,
I love a peerless woman,
and savor the moments in which
I can converse about her with someone
who shares my endearment.

In the Meantime

Like clockwork,
I find you again,
dozing in your burgundy chair,
perched between dreams and reality,
the leather cradles you
long after dark has descended.
Wonder sprouts:
Why not bed?

Like clockwork,
you rise on a schedule
that even the sun is late for,
peeling limberly from the sheets
as your dreams stir,
grasping the chance to nestle
in your mind's innovation cavities.
Aren't you worn?

Yet you do not yearn for lazy afternoons,
basking in lack of responsibility:
Intuitive Living,
each whim guiding the next
in an integrated web of self-satisfaction.
You thrive in integrity's presence,
finding virtue under every boulder
of opportunity,
scavenging the realms of equality
in hopes of truth,
never shunning with trepidation
of possibility,
and how far it can extend.

The leather grasps you,
cools your inspired skin,
tired from titillation,
your ideas ooze form the pores.
Between reality and dreams,
you choose to stay,
finding light for others
behind half-lidded eyes,
never allowing your brain to truly sleep,
eventually embracing bed only out of custom
and expectation.
You hope to give more, create more,
change more,
even in battle between
your body's weariness
and your mind's everlasting will to inspire.

And you rise early,
your body following suit
to your mind's ambition,
sacrificing hours on the clock
usually designated for sleeping
and living by your own clock,
your inner clock,
the early morning's shadows
no less of an inspiration for progress
than your naps in the burgundy chair.
You create your own timetable
to sustain your everlasting flow of ingenuity,
living completely by your intrinsic mantra:
There are never enough hours.

How to Find the Remote Control

-Prerequisites:
a) Be my father, John.
b) Have a wife, Julie, and three daughters.
c) Name them (in chronological order) Ried, Sloane, & Mycah.

Begin:

1) Be left alone in the house all day on a Saturday.

2) Despite being the literal man of the house, embrace your temporary position as Man of the House by taking control of all domains conquered by your family (a bossy group, obviously inheriting strong opinions from their mother).

3) Dedicate the day to "John-Friendly" activities, filling the morning with your daughters' overdue chores.

4) Upon noticing your wife's persistently growing pile of dirty laundry in the bedroom corner, reorganize your closet too.

5) Feel fulfilled after regaining order of the possessions around you, ignoring the irony of your (lone) affinity for cleaning despite traditional gender roles.

6) Decide to take a break as your thoughts drift to the contents of the refrigerator.

7) Go to the kitchen and make yourself a roast beef sandwich, because you can with Julie out of the house, unable to glare and refer to it as "heart-attack beef".

8) After you have devoured the sandwich over the sink, decide your exciting morning has earned some relaxation and relocate to the family room.

9) Decide to watch T.V., despite your years as an educator and advocate of reading in your children's lives. No one comes between you and the All-Westerns-all-the-time-Channel.

10) Momentarily remember telling your children to "go pick up a book" every time you discovered them in front of the television.

11) Also remember those book reports you started assigning when they were in 1st grade.

12) Feel slightly hypocritical.

13) Wonder if a baseball game is playing, perhaps the Chicago Cubs.

14) Cry inside, but only for a moment, over the sheer incapability of the Cubs to pull it together.

15) Recompose yourself and think optimistically- at least you have passion, even if it is for a chronically disappointing team.

16) Wonder where the remote control is.

17) Actually, wonder where "The Clicker" is, because that is what you think it is called.

18) Glance around, hoping for a flash of The Clicker's shiny surface.

19) Glance longer, thinking maybe your age has affected the former agility of your eyes.

20) Begin to get heated, although prematurely, seeing as you've barely looked for one minute.

21) Look under the couch cushions, under the pillows, and under the furniture.

22) Have severe difficulty with the previous task (considering your soon-to-be retirement and large, stocky frame) and cease searching after a few moments.

23) Conclude that one of your daughters, the chronic T.V.-watchers, must be the culprit behind the missing Clicker.

24) Hear the side door to the house slam, indicating the return of one of the suspects.

25) Take advantage of this opportunity to interrogate the returnee, hoping to uncover the Clicker's whereabouts.

26) Shout, "Hello!" and wait for a reply, identifying the voice without having to change locations.

27) Hear from the other room, "Hey Padre" and realize by the nickname it's your youngest, Mycah.

28) Call, "Mycah, Come here now!" in your frustrated-but-not-quite-angry-yet voice.

29) Leave her wondering if she'd done something meriting a talking-to or "vision talk", your umbrella term for all disciplinary conversations.

30) Stay confident that your potential shift to angry-voice still strikes the "Fear-of-God" into her heart, as when she was 5 years old.

31) Let her realize that she cannot remember doing anything wrong but still heed your call, reveling in this confirmation of your fatherly efficacy.

32) Start your inquisition out strong with, "Mycah, where the fuck did you put The Clicker??"

33) Don't wait for a response before pointing fingers wildly, stating "YOU were the one that had it last!"

34) The fact that you have absolutely no evidence to back up your last statement does not cross your mind, as you look stern and continue to bellow about The Clicker nonsensically.

35) Notice that your daughter is yelling back but you cannot hear her over your own.

36) Catch a few phrases of her speech: "I haven't watched T.V. in two days!"; "Did you check under the couch cushions?" and finally, "Sloane was in here this morning."

37) Think to yourself, *Aha! Sloane WAS in here this morning! She'll know!*

38) But say to Mycah, "Yeah right, you probably hid it from me!" just to be difficult.

39) Begin helping as she searches the room.

40) Hear the door slam again, interrupting your thoughts.

41) Watch Mycah run to greet the next suspect, shouting "Hey, who is that? Come in here!" before she can reveal you intentions of interrogation.

42) Recognize Sloane's voice as you overhear her ask Mycah, "What did I do?"

43) Bark out, "Sloane! Come in here right now!" your patience waning at her less hasty reaction than Mycah.

44) Notice that her face looks mildly annoyed, mounting your frustration further by her lack of understanding of the severity of your dilemma.

45) Avert to your initial tactic of accusing before she can refute, shouting "Where the hell did you put The Clicker??"

46) She begins to respond ("I didn't put it anywhere…") and interrupt with the familiar, "YOU were the one who had it last! You were watching T.V. this morning!"

47) Think you've caught her with this fact, until she replies, "Yes, and I set it on the coffee table."

48) Swivel around to the coffee table with frenzied hope in your eyes, only to discover what your "search" concluded- the Clicker is no longer on the coffee table.

49) Scream at your daughters in frustration, "Well where the hell did it go! If it's not on the table, where is it? What could have possibly happened to it between this morning and now?"

50) Watch as they both shrug their shoulders and ponder your previous questions.

51) Pause to wipe your now severely sweaty head (you are bald, tending to get sweaty and red during intense moments).

52) Scream again, "Well come on! Help me look!"

53) Instruct your offspring to tear the room apart, a flash of jaded exasperation in their eyes reflecting past experience with misplaced Clickers, car keys, etc.

54) Hear the door slam a third time as your wife Julie enters the house calling, "Hello?"

55) Wait for her to discover the family's whereabouts, aware that your plight is about to be exposed.

56) Upon discovery, hear her ask, "What are you guys doing in here..." in clear confusion, unaware of how to spin the situation to your advantage.

57) Stand speechless amidst pillows, blankets, and coffee-table books that are now strewn about the room.

58) Listen as Sloane informs her, "We're looking for the remote," before returning to her scavenging.

59) Continue to stand still, as Julie enters the room and begins searching as well, starting with the coffee table.

60) Watch as she shuffles a pile of magazines on the table, the same pile you decided was unnecessary to "search", topped with what should have been a surprising item for the current technology, a VHS tape.

61) Watch in almost slow motion as she picks up the box, realizes that it does not contain a tape but isn't empty, and The Clicker slides out onto her palm.

62) Feel a sudden rush a fury, exploding "HOW THE HELL DID THAT GET THERE?" in sweaty exasperation.

63) Suddenly remember what you were doing before you decided to watch T.V.

64) Remember your attempt to clean earlier led you to dust the furniture.

65) Realize that while dusting the furniture you removed everything from the antique, wooden coffee table, which had been in grave need of dusting.

66) Realize those 2 hours ago, you compiled that pile of magazines and placed the tape box on top, hoping to inquire about the whereabouts of its missing contents later.

67) Realize that in this compilation, you must have been the one to "hide" The Clicker.

68) Mycah: "I didn't put that there."

69) Sloane: "I didn't put that there."

70) Julie: "I didn't put that there."

71) Watch as they all turn to look at you.

72) Attempt to be casual, "Huh, well would you look at that."

Chapter Five – Politics as Usual

These seven poems are offered as a statement about the state of the world and my interaction with that world.

The focus for the seven follows:

- "Lincoln's Birthday" – history and the present merge together.

- "I Am Better" – facing death of a loved one.

- "Who Am I" – a supercharged place for commitment to real change.

- "New Cues" – embracing the merging of the new with the stability of the old.

- "The Question Is" – finding the depth to take on the politics of the world?

- "A Sea Change" – a four-hundred-year quest achieved on the first Tuesday of November 2008.

- "Home" – a kind of epitaph.

Lincoln's Birthday

A memory
of a great man.
A man who died
so others could live.

His greatness
is not because of politics,
But rather, his greatness
is because of love.

He agonized
over how to free
a nation of its hate,
and yet generated hate too.

He prayed
for the wisdom,
wisdom from a God
he did not know existed.

He wept
because of death,
death practiced
to create life's opportunity.

I Am Better

I give you this one thought to keep –
        I am with you still.
I do not sleep.
        I am not gone –
I am with you still
        with each new dawn.

Therefore, I need your voice,
        ever stronger.
As age accumulates,
        I cannot turn away
           from your presence.
I am better because you were.

Who Am I

Who am I?
Am I brilliant?
Courageous,
Talented,
Fabulous.
"Actually, who am I not to challenge me so?"

New Cues

New cues of love,
New frames,
New wine,
Old bottles.

Old antiques,
Old house,
Love renewed
Again and again.

The Question Is...

Will the words come again?
Will the window to my intellect open?
Will I be able to redefine my meaning?
Will the flow be there to express my soul?

I do not always feel the flow.
At times it seems the words are stuck,
unable to find their way to my fingers
and jumbled within my mind's eye.

I sometimes feel the flow without the urges,
unmoved to clarify what I am thinking,
bogged down with multiple outlines,
unable to put forward coherent thoughts.

When the words come,
I am transparent. Thoughts come
out of mind to my physical conveyor belt,
springing onto paper.

The question is can I control the flow,
control the time and the timing
by intellectually and emotionally
tapping the window to my soul?

A Sea Change

We watched in disbelief.
Could he really win?
Could a black man really become our President?
Could our fellow citizens put away
their biases and prejudices?

And then we knew he could,
but could he turn red states blue?
Was his ground game strong enough
to win Ohio, then Virginia,
and then the West – Nevada, New Mexico?

Oh my God, what was happening?
Even Indiana, the red of the red
or could it be? Florida –
Florida where the election of 2000
was stolen – now blue.

Ah, but the ultimate – North Carolina
has now gone blue too.
And together with Iowa, Pennsylvania,,
Wisconsin, Minnesota, and Michigan
too along with that old stalwart New Hampshire
The map of the United States is rewritten.

A sea change for me.
    With Obama,
a sea change for us.
We are a new country!

Home

I am going home today.
Now that's some place
I have never been.

Chapter Six – Personal Introspection

The world is perfect. However the 'is' is the way the world is supposed to be. There is no stress in the world. There is no catastrophe in the world. What adds stress and catastrophes and flaws to the world is our own reflections, interpretations, and introspections.

The following poems offer the story of a man working through his reflections, interpretations, and introspections. Pain and joy show through.

The View from Nearby

What do I see
as I look nearby?
Is my sight expansive,
or restricted by shortsightedness?

I am not certain
whether my view
captures nuances
of the picture before me.

I am surprised by neglected
first looks,
when I take time
to look again.

The nooks, corners, and transparencies
available through new eyes
strike my worldview,
forcing me to reflect anew.

So, what I see nearby
expands, with the help
of those within the circle
of ever-expanding life.

Recycle

Meandering deliberately,
slowly turning,
spying the sliver of light
watching reflections of every hue.

Drifting mindfully,
twirling each thought
drawing the essence
inwardly experiencing each Word.

Startled suddenly
by reality's presence
pain, suffering, death
lurking just around the edges of my mind.

Words take on meaning,
connect to thought patterns
driving explosive action
no longer lingering, but twisting at right angles.

Adrenalin flows
pupils, ears, and muscles tense
a new leaf emerges from the old
an old leaf floats away.

Looking Back

Looking forward to tenseness ending for a day.
Right now, my shoulders and thoughts
have overtaken
  my wants and desires.
Caught in responsibility trap, looking to
  spring free – I will be free.

Free, floating backwards to another
  day and time.
Listening to the small voice of a giving boy
  running after Shep the faithful collie,
  looking for Blackie, the cow
    on top of Old Smokie.

Never did get that lake built Dad.
We missed the biggest trout in the stream
  on that cold May morning.
We missed him, but caught our freedom,
  freedom to love.

We forgot to touch that last piece of floating
  life down that stream.
Dad, I miss you and I cherish
  those memories, moments of freedom.
Dad you are one hell of a man.

Revisiting each stage of life.
Sorting through the acts of volition
  Letting go of the present
Flooding the mind with my past
Preparing for a better day to come.

Lengthening of Days

How do I know if I am ready?
Dry bones of my past.
How did I know I was ready?
Did I always know?
Did I never really know?
Did I know sometimes?
Dry bones of my past answer?

Choice,
when these days lengthen,
and their number totals a precious few,
what am I choosing to do
    with the leftover time?
Are my choices known to me now?
Am I in control and will I be ready?

Ready for the ending of days.
ready for choice to end,
and satisfied with the fulfillment of days.
Do I have a direction?
Am I ready?
Can I accept?
Have I come to terms with turning to stone?

Flow

Flow. Flow with life itself.
Be not tied to the mortgage
be not forced into compromise
in the name of security.
Be not a part of the lie
be not unwilling to face yourself.
Be not afraid
of the connectedness of change.
Be not fearful of the new
nor hateful of the old.

Rather be.
Be the sky, the ocean
the lifting tune, the shifting weight,
the warm fragrant flower.
Be all that ever was or ever will be.
When you have experienced it all,
just flow into the moment,
embracing one more experience
just because it's there.
Flow, Be.

Unique Too

We are the sum total of all our experiences.
We are the floating heights of a cloud,
we are the crashing fall of a waterfall,
we are the instantaneous smile of a child,
we are the growling sound of a trapped animal,
we are the pounding of a fist
    in anger and anguish,
we are the awesome energy of a first love,
we are all of these disparate things,
and yet, we are each unique too!

The Answer

I ache.
I look at the foolishness of all that
surrounds me.
I ask, "Is it all still worth it?"
Is anything worth this much pain?
And what the worst of it is –
I don't know
the answer.

Truth, Welcome

I am the center of the universe and time now.
 I feel all that has ever been
 welling up inside me,
   and ready to burst forth into all I ever can be.
I thirst for my truth.
 I ache to discover it.
I am becoming my truth,
     feeling it powerfully in my loins.
Truth! Welcome

Child of the Universe

I am a child of the universe,
seeking connections with that universe,
understanding naught, but seeking all
there is to find.

I blithely seek the comforts of a woman,
touch the soft fur of a cat,
view the lovemaking of an insect,
and wonder who has viewed all of this before.

I encourage the revelation of mystery
in life and eagerly ask why
that is the way that it is.
I am a child of the universe – I am the universe.

Alive

I am the God of hellfire
I am the exploding mountain
I am the flight by the mystic bird
I am the essence of the universe.

I am all of these things
I am much more
I am fully aware as a human being
I am alive!

Looking

Looking for a way of expressing what I feel
Looking for words that will communicate
Looking for the symbols to paint my soul
Looking, looking, looking.

Eternal Sea

Washing waves over my soul
I listen to the hypnotic call
I search out the historical story,
appreciating the eternal nature.

Washing waves over my footprints,
I view the deeply held blueness,
I see the sparkling treasure,
blessed with a bit of wonder.

Washing waves touching my roots,
I sense your part in my part,
I relate to your moistness in my veins,
understanding that I too am eternal.

The Mountaintop

Words I speak are absorbed.
Some connections,
some understanding,
some sense of acknowledgement.

Perhaps some connectedness with the soul,
the soul of the living,
and those emerging in the future.
We just might make it to the mountaintop.

I Seek

I seek out the inner me,
to know this person.
I search for the core,
wondering in awe at the thought I produce.
I am amazed by the flow of my world.
I reminisce about my past creations,
anticipating my future frustrations.
What is my soul saying to me?

I Want

I want to soar higher than ever before,
stepping into tomorrow
experiencing the unexperienced
Touch the untouched, grasp the fleeting

I want to become aware of my entire being
I want to seek and expose inner spaces,
to understand the misunderstood,
Encounter the unencountered, seek mystery.

I want to concentrate on achieving full intimacy,
to connect with another soul
I want to love the unloved,
Embrace the unembraced, capture the heart
 of another life.

I want to know the source of knowledge
I want to learn the essence of existence
I want to study the unstudied,
Acknowledge the unacknowledged,
complete the investigation
 of my meaning of our world.

Self Portrait

Capable, concerned, caring,
touching, competitive
misunderstood.
petty, knowledgeable
loving, lonely, crying!

Why do I wander so far
into unchartered territory?
Because I must know what I am,
who I am, and why I am –
 a searcher.

Song to Me

Torture, separation, isolation.
All words, but with special meaning
in the life of a loner.

Words representing the evening
spent searching for their definitions,
wishing for union.

Time passes.
The world changes,
but the solitary self acknowledges naught.

What enters the psyche
doesn't promote growth,
but holds out as lost vision.

Vision of perfection,
or chaos?
Each one dependent on the other.

The question is
will the solitary self
choose perfection? Or chaos?

Hello

"From now on things are goin' to be different,"
from a song.
I love it but I don't embrace the differences.
I am going to learn to live wide open
and concerned about enjoying all around me
at every moment.

Boredom, you have met your match –
I welcome the challenge of life
up close and personal.
What I do, I know I do well, and
I will continue those actions.
What I cannot do, I shall work at
learning how.

When I get angry, I will make an effort
to step back and realize
Generally I create the conditions that lead
to my anger.
Therefore,
I will assert what I need clearly
and enunciate more clearly what
I can give.

I shall be the closest I can
to what I want to be –
I embrace all that is there and
welcome it in. Hello.

The Continuum

I have been here before,
I remember the sounds.
I have drunk this cup of tea before,
written these words before,
felt the blood rush through my veins before,
and listened to my heart before.

All this I have done before,
yet it is brand new,
captured for eternity
by the scratching on paper,
but still unique
in its moment of existence.

Sounds heard
will never be so heard again,
eternity, momentary,
sameness and uniqueness,
the same on the continuum.

Mortality

I am alone in this world
I must ultimately decide
I am the controller of my fate
I decide the direction.

As I approach my inner core,
I must step into that core
and experience its horrors,
Its disbeliefs.

I must confront the awful secrets
resting below the surface.
I must determine to ride out
my storm of hypocrisy.

I must grip my insecurities
squeeze them until I understand.
Face being alone,
accept the actuality of my own mortality.

Listen to Your Heart

The moment I listened to my heart,
sounds invaded my thoughts,
so clearly unique to the moment,
but warning of world yet to come.

A world yet to come when fear subsides,
where anxiety slips into oblivion,
where our nerves don't jangle ,
but instead they vibrate with pieces
of the Heart.

Pieces of the heart emerge!
Emerge to touch the emotive being,
emerge to clasp the I to the thou,
but even so, there are mysteries!

Mysteries of the love anew,
love so heartfelt,
love enthralling,
and love so crystal pure, everlasting.

Listen to your heart and you too will hear
the sound of your life's story,
unfolding with possibility,
meaning the Moment!